FASTING
and Prayer

FASTING and *Prayer*

Obedience to **GOD** and **Other Victories**

YOLANDA T. AMON

Copyright © 2019 Yolanda T. Amon.

Cover Photo Credits:
Makeup Clare Amon
Photo Credit Surah Amon

Dedication Scriptures

"JESUS said unto them, My meat

is to do the will of him that sent

me, and to finish his work"

(John 4:34).

"For man shall not live by bread alone

but by every word that proceedeth

out of the mouth of GOD"

(Matthew 4:4).

"And I will restore to you the years that

the locust hath eaten, the cankerworm,

and the caterpillar, and the palmer worm,

my great army which I sent among you"

(2 Joel 2:25).

Contents

Surrender and Receive Victories

The Almighty GOD must be calling you to fast, and I'm not sure why. What I mean is, everybody's calling, journey and walk with GOD is different. Therefore, I don't know exactly why HE wants you to fast, but according to Jeremiah 29:11, HIS plans are to prosper you and not harm you, but to give you a future and a hope (Jeremiah 29:11).

The above scripture describes GOD'S plans for you. It says that HIS plans for you are good plans that will cause you to prosper and have a future and hope. Getting to know GOD and seeking HIS plans for your life is a step in the right direction, and will change your life for the better.

Another scripture that encourages you to fast is found in Luke 4:4. It says that man cannot live by bread alone but by every word that proceedeth out of the mouth of GOD. Our LORD and SAVIOR, JESUS CHRIST gave this answer to satan when he tried to tempt HIM after HE had been fasting for forty days. This scripture lets us know that there will be times when natural food won't be appropriate, because man also needs spiritual food, which is the word of GOD.

I heard someone talking about good health and high performance. They mentioned superfoods like moringa, spirulina, wheatgrass and kale, but GOD has said to us that we cannot live on bread alone, but by every word that proceeds out of

HIS mouth. This means that even if you take all of the "superfoods", you would not be as strong as you would be if you had the proper balance of GOD'S WORD and natural food. It is written, the joy of the LORD is our strength (Nehemiah 8:10).

Let's look at the clues that we have based on HIS word so that we understand why HE is calling us to fast.

2Chronicles7:14 says if my people who are called by my name, shall humble themselves and pray, seek my face, and turn from their wicked ways then will I hear from heaven, and will forgive their sins, and will heal their land. The humbling that is referred to in this scripture is fasting. The book of Ezra confirms this.

Ezra 8:21 then I proclaimed a fast, there, at the river at Ahava, that we might humble ourselves before our GOD, to seek from him the right way for us and our little ones and all our possessions.

Quite possibly, there are things in you, or in your life that are hindering you from getting the victories that GOD has planned for you. It could be spirits of pride, rebellion or disobedience. These spirits can keep you away from GOD and keep you doing your own thing, when HE only wants what's best for you.

GOD says in HIS word, that HE gives grace to the humble, but HE resists the prideful. Remember the scripture says that after pride, comes the fall and that disobedience is as the spirit of witchcraft. If the spirits of pride and disobedience are in you, they will keep you from drawing close to GOD. Consequently, you won't get the help that you desire and need. However, these spirits can be exposed, subdued, and cast out by fasting and prayer. This could be the reason why GOD wants you to fast and pray.

In general, God desires to give you life, and life more abundantly (John 10:10). We know that based on Ephesians 3:20, HE is able to do exceedingly and abundantly above all that we could ask or think according to the power that works in us. This means that whatever you think that you will gain from fasting, you will gain that and more. Hallelujah! Your surrender is going to lead to more victories than you expected!

We have identified four facts concerning the reason why GOD wants you to fast based on HIS word.

1. HE wants to give you a future.

2. HE wants you to give you hope.

3. HE wants to heal your land. This can be taken literally or figuratively. For example, most nations need their land healed from one sin or the other. Unless otherwise led by the Precious Holy Spirit, look at it as referring to the certain areas of your life that need healing. There may be something in you, or in your life that is trying to stop you from having a victorious life. This can be turned around by drawing nearer to GOD, and away from the thing or things that are prohibiting you

from having a closer relationship with HIM.

4. HE is able to perform exceedingly and abundantly above what you are expecting according to the power that works in you. GOD can do more for us than we can do for ourselves.

Those are four motivating reasons to surrender and fast.

Here are some signs that GOD wants you to fast and draw nearer to HIM

1. You are reading this book.

2. You feel by spiritual instinct, that it's time for you to fast.

3. HE wakes you up between 3am and 5am. However, it could be another time, but more than likely, it will be at the same time every day. I won't put GOD in a box, because HE has different ways of doing things, and HE customizes HIS care, and our walk with HIM.

4. Every time you are on your way to engage in a negative behavior, you feel a very strong "no" in your spirit. The behavior could be sexual, it could be eating, or it could be associating with bad company. It could even be allowing yourself to be distracted by social media.

GOD has given you signs. It's no longer a doubt in your mind that you need to fast and pray, to seek the LORD'S direction. The LORD will be with you as HE guides you into victory. It's normal to wonder how to start, but the way to start is already in your heart.

What has GOD told you to give up for years? What has HE told to deny yourself? Remember, victories can be won one step at a time. I know that you are ready for a positive change in your life, a change that leads to more than you expected. You are ready for major victories. It starts with surrendering.

Fasting and Praying is the Power Couple

Maybe you have been talking to GOD often, and that's what prayer is. It is talking with the Almighty. We hear many people talk about prayer. People even ask for prayer on social media. However, the Christian practice is not just prayer, but prayer and fasting. The body of Christ is being called back to fasting and prayer because it is the power couple. The Bible records how GOD responded when HIS people fasted and prayed.

The Book of Jonah

In the book of Jonah, GOD was going to destroy the city of Nineveh, because of the wickedness of the people. However, when the people fasted and stopped their wickedness, GOD spared the city.

Jonah 3:6 NIV When Jonah's warning reached the king of Nineveh, he rose from his throne, took off his royal robes, covered himself with sackcloth and sat down in the dust. This is the proclamation he issued by Nineveh: By the decree of the king and his nobles: Do not let people or animals, herd or flock taste anything; do not let them eat or drink

When GOD saw what they did and how they turned from their evil ways, he relented and did not bring on them the destruction he had threatened.

We know that GOD answers some prayers even if we are not fasting. But fasting and prayers go together. Oftentimes, fasting and prayers together will cause GOD to make major moves. Understandably, some people cannot fast because of health reasons. Therefore, I will add, food is not the only thing that GOD might ask you to give up or deny yourself for a period of time.

The Bible records so many victories won by the people of GOD by fasting and praying. JESUS CHRIST, our LORD and SAVIOR fasted and prayed for 40 days. After which,

HE responded to the devil with the word of GOD and the devil flew from HIM.

My obedience to GOD to fast, have prayer time and devotion to HIM for the last 9 months brought many victories for me.

1. In January of this year, I was 220pds. I currently weigh 140pds.

2. GOD birthed the spirit of sacrifice in me.

3. I am closer with HIM.

4. Now it's easier for me to submit my will to GOD'S will.

5. I am able to focus on the things in my life that GOD wants me to focus on.

6. Now, GOD'S Glory is being revealed in my life.

7. I was able to lead 3 people to CHRIST.

8. One person was healed from an issue of blood.

9. I was delivered from three ungodly spirits.

10. GOD answers my prayers of healings, and deliverance.

11. GOD elevated me spiritually and gave me more responsibilities.

12. GOD gives me ideals that will prosper me.

Fasting is a Part of our Christian Walk

If we really want to see victory in our lives, believers in Christ, have to fast and pray like we used to. When I came into holiness 10 years ago, we had to fast at least once or twice a year. Our main fast was the Daniel fast in January, and again mid-year around Pentecost. We were taught that fasting was a part of our spiritual walk.

I remember shortly after I had gotten saved, my Pastor called a fast. Oh my goodness, I did not want to fast. I was surprised that it was such a challenge for me because, when I was a Muslim, I would easily fast. However, in my Christian walk, fasting became challenging.

The church was on a fast and I didn't want to do it. One day, I decided that I wanted to eat fried chicken, instead of fasting so I went, and ate it. Boy was it good! However, when I returned home, the PRECIOUS HOLY SPIRIT of the living GOD, got right on my case. Once I returned home, I remember that an overwhelming desire to eat, to have sex, and anything else, came over me, all at the same time. My flesh was overtaking me, I had no self-control. And the PRECIOUS HOLY SPIRIT of the living GOD said to me, " IS THIS WHAT YOU WANT?" HE SAID, IF YOU DON'T FAST, YOU WON'T HAVE ANY SELF-CONTROL." Of course, after that encounter, I got right in line and started fasting. I pay that you learn from my testimony and not have to get in trouble before you can surrender to GOD.

Later, fasting became harder again because I wasn't practicing regularly. What I found to be true from experience is that GOD wants us to practice fasting regularly. It gives you self- control, and some spirits only come out by prayer and fasting (Mark 9:29).

Fasting as a Lifestyle

A fast can become a lifestyle, meaning that the things that you denied yourself temporarily, you don't go back to. A sister called me yesterday, and she told me that she had been fasting since July. She told me that she is not going back to the foods that she has been fasting from. She realized that they were not good for her anyway. Her fast became a lifestyle because she allowed GOD to set her on the right track.

GOD wants us to stay in a state of consecration, as opposed to going on a consecration. Consecrated means to be set apart for something holy. It does not make sense to live holy one month, and then go back to things that we know that are bad for us eleven months of the year. Most of the things that we consecrate from are of the world and are not good for us. Once GOD brings you out of ungodly behaviors, make up your mind not to revisit them.

For example, I used to drink processed sugary drinks. GOD put me on water and smoothies made of wheat grass, moringa, spirulina, fruit and vegetables. My plan is to never go back to pops and juices. I may drink juice or have pop from time to time. If I feel that I am getting out of control, I just make GOD a vow, and tell HIM, that I am denying myself a particular food or drink for a period of time.

Suppose GOD consecrated you from restaurant food. He could be trying to get you to stop spending too much money outside. HE could be trying to draw your attention to budgeting your money. Now obviously, you would be able to go to restaurants sometimes, but that's not something you should revisit on a regular basis. Personally, I save a lot of money by cooking my own food. The important concept here is that when GOD sets you on the right path, it becomes your responsibility to sustain it, and to even take it to the next level.

Another example; I used to eat a meal before going to bed, no matter how late I finished working. I would stop at a restaurant and get my favorite meal. Food was my comfort, instead of GOD. Boy, did HE break that habit! Now, I eat dinner around 4pm, and that's it! HE doesn't want me to eat another meal before I go to bed. This is a habit that I plan to keep.

I tried to break that habit on my own for decades, but I couldn't. This habit is gone now because GOD stepped in. I go to bed with HIM on my mind, or an assignment that HE has given me. Thank you, JESUS! Beloved, GOD will do the same for you, if you are obedient. HE is no respecter of persons (Acts 10:34-35).

Fasting and Prayer is the power couple. It really does get GOD'S attention. It gets HIM even more involved in your situation, problem or issue. Fasting and prayer together can make a difference in healings, deliverances, and cause GOD to change HIS mind, like discussed earlier in the book of Jonah.

The Bible as well as history, records that Queen Esther, called a fast to keep her people from being annihilated and it worked. This shows the power of prayer and fasting together. Can you think of any causes that you could fast and pray about? Most of us can. What about fasting and prayer to end violence, or for our loved ones to be delivered from substance abuse?

Prayer and fasting has always been a part of the Christian lifestyle. It helps you to develop self-control. It keeps you in a state of consecration so that you can always be used by GOD. It helps set you on the road to victory. People can be healed, delivered, and set free. GOD is calling us back to prayer and fasting.

Fasting and Losing Weight

It's no secret, many people want to fast to lose weight. Losing weight can be a good thing, especially when desired for health reasons and self-image. Everybody wants to feel good about themselves, this is normal.

Weight loss can help heal high blood pressure, diabetes and other illnesses and health problems. And the extra physical weight that we carry is sometimes a symptom of spiritual weights. The only way to know is to seek the LORD. Let's return to HIS way of prayers and fasting and get the victories in our lives!

But there are so many other benefits to fasting. GOD will exceed your expectations.

Chapter 3

What Foods Can You Eat When You Are on a Fast?

At the beginning of my fast, I ate boiled vegetables, brown rice, beans, nuts, and fruit. My meals did not look like a normal meal. I drank only water. This is because

GOD was birthing sacrifice in me. My meals were supposed to look like a sacrifice. Yours might be different, it will depend on what GOD is doing in you. From January to March, I ate very little meat. In April and May, HE allowed more foods but, HE also wanted me to begin making better food choices on my own.

Non restricted days mean I can eat what I want when I want. At first, I asked for three at the beginning of a new month. I would eat so much it would scare me and make me run back to fasting. I stopped asking for days off because I saw it as working against what GOD was trying to do in me. I try to stay away from foods, behaviors, people and places that are not good for me.

What do I eat on a regular day?

The foods that I eat can change from day to day. I can eat all things in moderation, except foods that I told GOD that I won't eat the rest of the year. These are food that I may tend to overeat. I generally eat a variety of fruits, vegetables, grains, nuts and beans. Remember, GOD will tell you what you should be eating. After prayers and devotion in the morning, I drink a smoothie or eat a piece of fruit and maybe some nuts and unsalted crackers with peanut butter. Remember, as you progress in your fast and journey, things will change. Your nutrition will change, your activities, behaviors, the people that you spend your time with and the places that you go, will all change. GOD has your attention.

I drink water until 4pm, and not too much water, or I will be too full to eat my meal. I try to eat sensibly for dinner. For example, I will eat two pieces of grilled chicken (without the skin), a baked potato and vegetables for dinner.

Meal Prepping is Very Helpful

Meal prepping was a very effective start for me. It helped me get on track with fasting and it helped to organize, and structure my life. In order to meal prep, I had to decide what I wanted to eat for the week ahead of time. I had to schedule time to grocery shop. I had to schedule time to cook. Then I had to repeat the process week after week. These things were done along with regular work hours, family time and scheduled prayers. I had no time to mess around. I became very focused.

After about twelve weeks of fasting, I had a revelation. I told GOD, "FATHER this is a great victory! I lost weight, I'm off my blood pressure medication. I saved quite a bit of money because I was preparing my own food. YOU and I are closer. I see that I can eat less food. I am focused on my life and goals, instead of being distracted. It's easier for me to fast and obey you." I was brought to tears.

The twelve weeks were a good exercise. It showed me how much I could get done for myself, by focusing and minding my own business. I was fasting, praying, and meal prepping, and focusing on my relationship with GOD for months. It was a time of "in reach," not "outreach." Glory Hallelujah! Thank You, JESUS!

Here are a couple recipes that you might enjoy

A Healthy Tasty Smoothie Recipe

1/3 to 1/2 of a small apple

1 celery stalk (with the leaf)

1 small banana

1 piece of ginger bark (about the size of a dime)

8 to 10 blueberries

1/4-1/3 cup of ice

1oz. of water

1 teaspoon (no more) of superfoods green powder, the one that I use contains moringa, spirulina, wheatgrass and Kale.

Blend or Juice and enjoy. This smoothie can be one or two servings.

Sweet Potato and Red Pepper Soup

1 large red bell pepper

2 medium sweet potatoes

½ can of tomato paste

1 garlic clove (chopped)

Salt

Black pepper

Jamaican pepper (optional)

Optional seasonings thyme, sage, curry

Chop garlic clove

Wash sweet potatoes (peel if you like), cut
   into squares not too small

Bring about 5 cups of water to a boil

Add to water sweet potatoes

Cut up red pepper and blend with ¼ cup
   of water and tomato paste

Add blended mixture to sweet potatoes

Season with garlic, salt and pepper

Cover and simmer on low for 30 mins.

At 3pm, if I'm not working, I pray until 4pm. This is so important because again, you are consecrating yourself from food (and anything else that GOD might tell you) but to GOD. At 4pm, I eat a reasonable dinner. It is challenging not to want to overeat at 4pm. Believe me, GOD will help you. I pray first, me and GOD'S relationship and agreement, is I put HIM before food. Natural food must never be first in my life again. I mainly eat vegetables, fish, chicken or beans, and sweet potatoes. I can eat cookies without crème. I told GOD that I will not eat anymore cake this year or drink any juice or soda pops. I drink water and smoothies. I plan to have a slice of cake on my birthday, January 10th, 2020.

God will let you know what you can eat on your fast. The key is to seek HIS direction and instruction. When HE gives it, do your best to be obedient. When and if you fall short, just turn from bad behavior and try again. Ask for forgiveness, GOD is merciful to forgive you again and again. Believe me, I messed up plenty of times, and GOD always forgave me.

After a while you may find that it wasn't what you were eating, it's what was eating you. You may get delivered while you are on this fast. It is written, some only come out by prayer and fasting (Matthew 17:21).

When you eat, it is a good idea to eat a variety of fruit and vegetables, beans and peas. As you continue to fast, you will begin to choose foods that you know have the nutrients that you need. Drink water unless GOD has told you to do a dry fast. Let go of foods that you know are not good for you like chips and too many sweets. Eat a variety of healthy foods, but your meals shouldn't be a feast. I try not to snack because, for me it is a sign of anxiety. Now, when I get the feeling to throw things in my mouth, I take a deep breath and disengage the trigger.

Remember, GOD may ask you to eliminate unproductive activities, behaviors, and or people from your life as well as certain foods. There will be an elimination of bad, distracting things and an increase of productive activities, behaviors and people in your life. If you have tendency to really get distracted, HE may want you to spend time away from certain people and activities until you realize what HE wants you to realize. He may tell you to set aside regular time for prayer and devotion. He is drawing you nearer to HIM so that you can receive directions that will lead you

to victories in your life and because GOD

likes spending time with us. HE loves us.

Chapter 4

Beloved, it's a Process

GOD has been working with me and you about our diets and obedience for years. HE will continue to work with us. HE wants to give us a future and a hope. First, HE will eliminate things from your diet and your lifestyle, and then once you get use to fasting and it becomes easier for you, you will begin to do it. For example, when I began fasting in January, no sugary drinks were allowed. I drank one pop this year, on a day that I wasn't fasting. Otherwise, I haven't had any processed sugary drinks this year. I can't see any reason to start back drinking sugary drinks. It wouldn't make any since. I went without them for months, they are eliminated from my diet permanently.

Soon you will agree that FATHER, indeed knows best. I remember when I first started having problems with my blood pressure. GOD started taking things out of my diet.

Potato chips were the first thing to go. Most of us have a favorite potato chip, but we cannot let potato chips kill us. I'm so serious. We cannot let food and disobedience kill us. We have too much to live for. We must live for our children, ourselves, and the other lives connected to our lives.

In the beginning, it will be challenging to be around food and not be able to eat. Soon, that will be a thing of the past. You will be able to walk in a grocery store and not be overcome by the food, which is a great accomplishment. To overcome this trigger, I would declare and decree that I am not subjected to my environment, but my environment is subjected to me. I had to constantly declare this, but I overcame that trigger.

Years ago, GOD put me on an eating schedule with no snacking in between. For years I stuck with it, but slowly I began to overeat, even though I was eating on a schedule.

Fasting helps the body to get used to smaller portions, because it makes the stomach shrink. I was feeling like I need to finish entire meal. However, I learned to put my food aside, and come back to it later. I still need help with certain areas pertaining to food and eating. GOD knows and HE will help me. Thank you JESUS! Hallelujah! What a mighty GOD we serve. I'm telling you, you will look back and your testimony will be that so many victories were won from your obedience.

The Spirit of Sacrifice

We hear the people of GOD; talk a great deal about the power of prayer, but not so much about fasting anymore." We use to say, "push your plate back." During those times, there was a spirit of sacrifice that rested on the people of GOD, which caused them to push their plates back. For example, someone needed to be saved, or somebody needed to be healed. The church would come together and fast and pray until they saw results. There were things going on that they felt was worth pushing their plates back for. There even more things going on now but the problem is many people don't have the spirit of sacrifice. That's one of the things that GOD may birth in you through fasting.

Can you think of anything going on in your life or family that would be worth missing a meal for? Does anybody need to be healed, saved, or delivered from drugs or perversion? Most people's answer to that question would be yes. I pray that GOD births a spirit of sacrifice in you. Take the first step which is obedience. Only you know what GOD is telling you to do.

Grace and Mercy for Where You Are Right Now

You might be thinking, how can you sacrifice and fast for others when you can't do it for yourself? Beloved, it's process. Whatever you desire, it will not happen overnight. But it might. Our GOD does instant miracles to increase the faith of "babes in CHRIST" or new believers. (John 2:11). You could be in line for a instant miracle. The question is if GOD can do that one miracle for you, what else can HE do for you? I'm telling you, GOD can fix your entire life!

GOD has to birth some things in you and take some things out of you. This takes time. The beautiful thing is GOD will meet you where you are right now. You can come to Him just as you are, and HE will start the process. His grace and mercy will meet you and carry you all the way to victory.

Let's pray, FATHER, in the name of JESUS, help us, please LORD. FATHER, many of us are over-eating to cover something else. Or we may be eating foods that don't agree with our digestive systems. FATHER, please intervene. YOU birthed fasting in me. Father in the name of JESUS, what people see in my life is your work, your Almighty hand. Father have mercy on your people.

FATHER, replace bad habits with good habits. FATHER, have mercy on us, don't let our enemy triumph over us. Nobody loves us like YOU do, nobody cares for us like YOU do. FATHER, in the name of JESUS, you are the GOD who wants to give us a future and a hope. FATHER, I cry out for myself and for your people today.

FATHER, nobody can meet a person where they are like you can. LORD, please help us.

56

Break every unprofitable habit and replace them with habits that will lead us to your original plans for our lives. Father whatever it is, we ask that you break it, in the Mighty Name of Jesus. FATHER, I will give your name all the praise, all the honor and all the glory.

Chapter 5

Obedience

I'm writing this book to encourage you to follow the lead of the precious HOLY SPIRIT, consecrate yourself from the world, and to GOD. Remember, if you stop one activity, you will need to replace it with another activity. For example, when lunch was eliminated from my diet, I replaced it with reading the Bible. That does not mean that GOD will tell you to do the same thing. HE might tell you to pray or take a walk. The key is to be obedient to whatever HE says.

I didn't set out to lose weight, I set out to be obedient to GOD and get back to my special place with GOD. However, I looked up and I had lost 80 lbs., and many other victories. Of a truth, GOD can do more for you than you can do for yourself. Just trust HIM and be obedient.

Do you want to be healed, delivered and set free? What has GOD called you to do and what are the secret desires of your heart? What are some negative things in your life that are trying to defeat you? Your obedience to GOD can set your life on the right track and get you many victories.

The story of Ruth in the Bible is a testimony of how being obedient can turn your life around for the better. Her history was discouraging until she decided to follow a woman of GOD, her mother-in-law, Naomi back to Bethlehem. Both women's husbands had died and left them with no children and no money. Ruth loved her mother-in-law, and she swore that she would never leave her. She even left her country and family and followed her back to Bethlehem.

Naomi heard that GOD had blessed his people with bread in Bethlehem. They both went to Bethlehem, Naomi and Ruth. Ruth began to work in the field of Naomi's older, wealthy relative, Boaz. When Naomi knew that Ruth had obtained favor with Boaz, she gave her instructions about how to win his heart. Ruth did exactly what she was told. She was obedient to her mother-in-law and did not despise her instruction. And her obedience set her life on a winning track forever!

Ruth went from being a poor widow, to a wealthy wife. She became the great grandmother of the beloved King David, which put her in the lineage of our LORD and SAVIOR JESUS CHRIST.

Ruth was obedient and followed her mother in law's instructions and won the heart of Boaz. The wealthy, anointed, holy Boaz married Ruth and changed her life. One act of obedience set her life back on track forever.

Don't Miss Your Blessings, Lead not to Your Own Understanding

In 2Kings 5:10, there is the story of a man who almost missed his healing because he didn't think that the instructions that he was given made since. He thought that it would take more for him to be healed than it did. But all it really took was his obedience.

Naaman was a commander of the Syrian army. The Syrian King held him in great esteem because of the victory that GOD brought him. The Bible said that he was a mighty man of valor; a man with strength, courage and passion. He had a wife, and servants. His life was together, except for one thing. Naaman had a disease called leprosy. This disease causes the skin to turn white and people who had this disease were considered unclean. When the King of Syria was told that the GOD of Israel, could heal Naaman, he sent Naaman there to be healed.

Naaman had an image in his mind of how his healing would take place. Because of this image, he almost missed his healing. He thought that Elisha, the Prophet, would come out to meet him, call upon the name of the LORD, lay his hands on his body and he would be healed. That was not GOD'S plan. Instead, the prophet Elisha sent a messenger to Naaman and told him to go and wash himself in the Jordan River seven times. Naaman begin to rationalize and doubt the instructions that he was given. He thought that the rivers of Damascus would be better to wash in than the Jordan River. He even walked away in a rage. Thank GOD, His servants came near to him and advised him to heed the instructions of the prophet, finally he obeyed and was healed!

Naaman thought that his healing required more than it really did. But it only required his obedience. The healing was the one thing that he needed to make his life complete, but it depended on his obedience. After he was healed, He proclaimed that there is no GOD in all the earth, but in Israel

What's on your mind? What's bothering you? What is it that you think you have to do to get what you want? Enough of what you thought it took, or what you heard other people say you have to do to get what you want! Whose report will you believe today? Believe the report of the LORD! Take the first step of obedience and watch what GOD will do!

Let's pray, FATHER in the name of JESUS, FATHER, we thank you and we praise you for who you are and for what you have done. FATHER, so many of us cannot take another step because of what we heard. We have heard so many negative things, so many hard things, but FATHER, your way is light, your yolk in light. FATHER, I ask this in your son JESUS' name that you stop the warfare in your people's minds. Remove worry, fear doubt, give us another chance FATHER. Give your people a heart that can and will respond to you FATHER, as you give them instructions that will set them free and set their lives on track.

FATHER, I ask these things in your son's JESUS, mighty name. Amen.

The bible teaches us to trust in the LORD with all our heart and lean not to our own understanding but in all our ways acknowledge HIM, and HE will direct our paths (Proverbs3:5-6). Just be obedient. You never know what GOD is up to, HE is always up to something bigger and better.

This book is meant to remind Christians that fasting as well as prayer is a part of our Christian lives. God expects HIS people to fast. In the book of Matthew, the disciples of John the Baptist asked Jesus, why is it that we and the Pharisees fast oft, but thy disciples fast not. And JESUS said to them, can the children of the bride chamber mourn, as long as the bridegroom is with them? But the days will come when the bridegroom shall be taken away from them, and then shall they fast.

In another instance, JESUS talks about how we should carry ourselves when we fast. He says that <u>when we fast</u>, not to look like the hypocrites of a sad countenance: for they disfigure their faces that they may appear unto men to fast. The point is that as believers of CHRIST, we are expected to fast.

Everything can be achieved by taking small steps. GOD will not expect you to start out on a three-day, dry fast or something that HE knows you can't handle. HE expects you to take small steps. Pray about it, and whatever HE tells you, be obedient. Your first instruction could be something very simple. Do it. It might not be what you expect, do it anyway. It's time for you to be healed and made whole. It's time for you to follow what is good for your life. Whether it's just one area of your life that you need help with or if you need GOD to fix your entire life, there are two things I'm certain about, one is HE is up for the challenge, and the second one is, your victory depends on your obedience.

Consecration as a Lifestyle

If you are a person that uses a detox program, you understand that there are some foods, behaviors that are poisonous to your life and future. In other words, you agree that these things are not good for you, yet you engage in them most of the year, but detox from them for thirty or forty days, then go back to them.

These are foods, behaviors, and or people, that feel good or taste good but their effects on your life and future is negative.

Once you start fasting, you deny yourself bad foods, behaviors, and bad company. You will start making healthier choices in all of those areas. You will realize that many of those things were actually bad for your life. Therefore, in a since you never come off the fast, but you receive a healthier, more productive lifestyle.

I look back on the last 10 months and I realize that the things that GOD consecrated me from were not good for me. This includes behaviors, some people, as well as foods. It makes since to stay away from these things, and to continue in the way of victory.

In the name of JESUS, we will no longer be robbed of eleven months of our lives and then live right, and sensible one month. This is where we will need courage, strength and wisdom.

Let's pray, Father in the name of JESUS, we are beginning to realize that the things that you consecrated us from were never good for us anyway. FATHER, please give us the strength and courage to keep doing the things that you told us to do and stay on the path of victory, in the mighty name of JESUS we have prayed.

We won't be able to keep this lifestyle by ourselves. We need GOD'S help. When I feel like my eating is getting out of control, I lean on GOD. What I mean is. I make HIM a vow. GOD has invested so much in all of us. HE hasn't failed us. I want to keep this testimony because so many people are being drawn to HIM because of it.

I noticed that my emotions would trigger me into eating. I began to disengage that trigger. I fight this by refusing to eat just because of an emotion that I am experiencing. When I feel like I'm eating too much of something, or I'm losing control. I lean on GOD. I say GOD, I will deny myself this food or this behavior. For me, when I say it to GOD, I get strength. One day, I ate a huge serving of cake. I knew that I had eaten too much. So, I said GOD, I'm not eating any more cake this year.

One of our neighborhood stores had slices of cake on sale for a dollar, I walked past that cake and said to myself, "I wouldn't care if that was a mountain of cake, I wouldn't touch it right now, because I said to my GOD that I will not eat cake the rest of this year. I maintain my lifestyle by leaning on my GOD.

Make an Agreement with GOD and Keep it

In the book of JOB 22:27-28 there are scriptures that are often partially used concerning making an agreement with GOD. The scriptures reads, Job 22:27 Thou shall make thy prayer unto HIM and HE shall hear thee, and thou shall pay thy vows. Verse 28 reads, thou shall also decree a thing, and it shall be established unto thee: and the light shall shine upon thy ways.

Many people just say, that they will declare and decree a thing, and it shall come to pass. However, based on the scripture, the ability to declare and decree is based on you keeping your agreement with GOD. There was a woman in the Bible who made an agreement or vow with GOD. Her name was Hannah, her husband's name was Elkanah, and he had another wife named Peninnah. She would tease Hannah and make fun of her because she didn't have any children. Hannah wept because of this and would not eat.

The family went up to worship yearly. Finally, one year, during worship, Hannah talked to GOD, and because of the way that she prayed, the priest thought that she was drunk. Her mouth moved but no words came out because she was praying in her heart. She was making an agreement with GOD, she told GOD, that if HE gave her a son that she would give him back to HIM to be raised in the temple. Remember, she had been praying and hurting for years, but nothing happened until she made

GOD a vow. It's really like making a deal with GOD.

GOD heard Hannah and answered her prayer. HE gave her a son. Hannah kept her vow to GOD, when she had weaned her son, she brought him to the temple to be raised in the house of GOD.

What's your issue, your problem? What do you need GOD to do? Talk to HIM about it. Beloved my prayer is that our relationships with GOD will be so strong that we get strength from HIM when we tell HIM what we want to do. And the agreement that we make with GOD is not a burden but an honor, in JESUS name. After all, GOD always keeps HIS word to us.

Our GOD honors agreements or vows. If we tell HIM something, we should try to keep our word. It's not always easy but it is a way for you to get strength and victory in your life. That's how I maintain a life of consecration. When I say to GOD that I'm not going to do something, I immediately get strength to keep my word. Sometimes, I fall short, I immediately apologize and then GOD forgives me. HE'S sweet, I know! If you fall short in an area, or can't complete a fast, just ask for forgiveness and strength and try again.

You have to have reverential fear for GOD to keep your agreement with HIM. Chances are Hannah would have wanted to bring up her son in her own home, but it was more important to her to keep her word to GOD.

Let's pray, Father right now in the name of JESUS, YOU are the GOD that honors vows. Even YOU GOD, YOU exalt your WORD above your name. FATHER, in the name of JESUS, we need that covenant keeping character. We need YOUR strength. We want to do what we say we are going to do FATHER. FATHER, if we say that we will fast, FATHER, please give us the strength and whatever it takes for us to honor our word.

FATHER, please give us whatever it will take to be able to stop unprofitable, ungodly behaviors. FATHER help us, we cry out to you, you are our help.

You are on the road to victory and you will keep going. Do your best to stay away from the foods, behaviors, activities, and people that you know are not good for you. Continue to practice the good habits that GOD has helped you form. And continue to draw nearer to him by having regular prayer times and devotion.

Continue to practice the good things. CONGRATULATIONS, YOU ARE ON THE ROAD TO VICTORIES!

Notes

Notes

Notes

Notes

Notes

Notes

Notes

www.ingramcontent.com/pod-product-compliance
Lightning Source LLC
Chambersburg PA
CBHW031356060726
47590CB00007B/2812